G000128587

BIRDS OF IRELAND

BIRDS OF IRELAND

This is a Tara Book
This edition published in 2000

Tara is an imprint of Parragon

Parragon
4 Queen Street House
Queen Street
Bath BA1 1HE, UK

Produced by Magpie Books, an imprint of
Constable & Robinson Ltd, London

Designed by Tony and Penny Mills

ISBN 1-902879-10-4

A copy of the British Library Cataloguing-in-Publication Data
is available from the British Library.

Printed and bound in China

CONTENTS

ALPHABETICAL LIST OF BIRDS

INTRODUCTION

Birdwatching is a hobby that can be pursued at many levels: you can put up a bird table or feeder and observe the species you attract from the warmth of your own home, or you can visit the coastal cliffs in winter or tramp the moors in spring and autumn. There will always be new species for you to see and new patterns of behaviour to understand.

It is the purpose of this book to whet the reader's appetite, to show the wide range and beauty of Irish birdlife, and to encourage an interest in a subject which is of ever-increasing importance if Ireland's natural heritage is to be preserved against the encroaches of modern life.

There is not space in a book of this size to offer comprehensive coverage. For further information, the Irish Wildbird Conservancy, which was formed in 1968 from an amalgam of several ornithological societies in Ireland, produces many books and an annual report, *Irish Birds*. The Birds of Ireland News Service gives information about rare sightings and unusual species.

Robin *Erithacus rubecula*   Spideog
The familiar 'red breast' of Christmas cards; often
unafraid of humans and easy to recognise with a
bright orange-red breast, which it employs as a
danger signal to other approaching Robins. Feeds on
insects, worms and seeds. Will often visit bird tables.
Where: Common all year round. Often found in
farmland and woodland.

House Sparrow *Passer domesticus*   Gealbhan binne
One of the commonest Irish birds and probably the
most widespread species in the world. Often found
in large, noisy flocks. They will take almost any
available food and have recently learnt from tits to
feed from nut feeders. A friendly and confident little
bird.
Where: Normally found close to human dwellings.
Resident all year round throughout Ireland.

Tree Sparrow *Passer montanus*   Gealbhan crainn
Very like the House Sparrow, but smaller and more
brightly coloured.
Where: It is found in woodland and farmland but
unlike its cousin it keeps well away from people.

**Robin (above)
and house sparrow**

**Wren (above)
and goldcrest**

Wren *Troglodytes troglodytes*   Dreoilín
A very small, busy bird, with a distinctive stubby, upright tail. Flight is short and low, with whirring wings. Feeds mostly on insects and spiders but can be attracted to bird tables. Suffers terribly in cold winters and its numbers can decline dramatically.
Where: Found all year round throughout Ireland, but prefers dense vegetation.

Goldcrest *Regulus regulus*   Ciorbhuí
The smallest bird in Europe. Often difficult to see; it is best to stand very still in a deciduous wood and try to locate it by its characteristic, very high pitched 'zeet' call. A very beautiful bird with a black bordered, bright yellow crest.
Where: Resident, but many migrants fly in annually from Britain and northern Europe. It is found mostly in woodlands but will also visit gardens.

Dunnock *Prunella modularis*   Donnóg
From a distance the dunnock can appear dull and drab, but a close examination will reveal beautiful patterning. It has a much thinner beak than the sparrow.
Where: Resident; found in gardens, woodland and farmland.

Coal Tit *Parus ater*   Meantán Dubh
The Irish Coal Tit is a separate species from the
British, with yellower cheeks, breast and belly and a
bigger build. When food is plentiful it will squirrel it
away. You can attract it to your garden bird feeder;
it enjoys seeds and fat.
Where: All year round, common in woods and
gardens.

Marsh Tit *Parus palustris*
Despite its name, it is mostly found in deciduous
woodland. It is very shy and unlikely to visit private
gardens or to use nest boxes. It is also rare and you
will do well to spot one.

Blue Tit *Parus caeruleus*   Meantán Gorm
A very common resident found in woodland, parks
and gardens. Blue-crowned head and bright yellow
breast with blue flashes on wings and tail.

Coal tit (above) and marsh tit

Great Tit *Parus major*   Meantán Mór

Another very common resident, found throughout Ireland. More often seen on the ground than other tits. It has a broad black band down its chest and can crack open nuts with its powerful bill. Like the Blue Tit, it will use a nest box if you put one up; it may, though, steal the cream from your milk bottle.

Long-tailed Tit *Aegithalos caudatus*   Meantán earrfhada

An active, gregarious bird. It has the smallest body of any Irish bird, with a tail over half its length. Acrobatic on the wing and agile on twigs, it feeds on small insects and spiders. Unlike other tits they do not nest in holes, but build oval, mossy nests in thorny bushes or high on trees.
Where: A common resident found throughout Ireland, it frequents woodland, hedgerows and gardens.

Siskin *Carduelis spinus*   Siscín

A very agile little finch which can hang on the most fragile twig to reach its food.
Where: A fairly common species found throughout Ireland, it breeds in coniferous woodland, but in winter it will spread to deciduous woodland in search of food; it has now also become a garden visitor.

Siskins (above)
and long-tailed tit

Bullfinch *Pyrrhula pyrrhula*   Corcrán coille
A very attractive, round little finch. Unfortunately it is
very unpopular with gardeners as it often strips off the
fresh buds from apple trees (up to thirty a minute).
Where: Common throughout most of Ireland, it likes
woods, orchards and gardens.

Chaffinch *Fringilla coelebs*   Rí rua
The plumage of the male is brighter in the summer
with a blue grey cap, a pink breast and brownish back.
They have a very strong bill which enables them to eat
grain and small seeds, but is sufficiently pointed to
take insects either in the air or from the ground.
Where: A very common resident found in gardens and
woodland.

Redpoll *Carduelis flammea*   Deargéadan coiteann
A small, dark finch, its back is brown with black streaks
and buff below, and it has a distinctive red patch on its
forehead. Its favourite food is seeds but it will take
insects.
Where: Resident; widespread throughout Ireland. It
nests in high bushes and conifers and, like the Siskin,
with whom it often associates, it will visit food tables in
town gardens.

Chaffinches

Brambling

Brambling *Fringilla montifringilla*   Breacán
A bright little finch with black and orange plumage
and a white rump. It often travels in huge flocks (it
was estimated seventy million were once gathered
round a beech wood in Switzerland). It feeds on
seeds and berries, but particularly enjoys beech mast.
Where: Although the commonest finch in northern
Europe, it is a rare winter visitor to Ireland. It can be
found in open fields and in woodland.

Linnet *Carduelis cannabina*   Gleoiseach
Like the Goldfinch, it was a popular caged bird in the
last century. It is a small bird with a chestnut back,
grey head and pink breast. It feeds on seeds and some
insects.
Where: A very widespread and common resident, it
can be found on farmland, waste ground and salt
marshes.

Blackbird *Turdus merula*   Céirseach

The male is most elegant, covered all over with glossy black plumage with an orange bill and yellow eye ring. It has an omniverous diet. It is highly territorial and will often engage in noisy disputes with visitors.
Where: A very common resident, found in gardens, farmland and woodland.

Song Thrush *Turdus philomelos*   Smólach

Has a distinctive speckled breast. Upper parts are a uniform brown and lack the range of colour of the larger mistle thrush. It is welcomed by gardeners as a favourite part of its diet are snails.
Where: Found all year round throughout Ireland in gardens, farmland and woodland.

Fieldfare *Turdus pilaris*   Sacán

A large thrush usually found in flocks. In the autumn its diet consists of berries and fruits including orchard windfalls. Later in the winter it will turn to worms and any insects it can find.
Where: A winter migrant from Scandinavia, favouring open fields and woodlands.

Fieldfares

15

Grey Wagtail *Motacilla cinerea*   Glasóg Liath
A cheerful little bird with a constantly wagging tail. Has a bright yellow breast, slightly paler in the female. It lives mostly on insects, but will also eat molluscs and sandhoppers.
Where: A common resident species, normally found close to swift-flowing rivers and streams.

Pied Wagtail *Motacilla alba*   Glasóg Shráide
A black and white bird with a long wagging tail. Although often found near water, they can be seen in drier places erratically chasing small insects on the ground, suddenly changing direction and wagging their tails the whole time.
Where: Like the Grey Wagtail, a widespread species found close to swift-flowing rivers and streams, but can also be seen in parks near ponds and lakes.

Yellow Wagtail *Motacilla flava*   Glasóg Bhuí
Males have a bright yellow chest and throat; females are slightly paler. Found in marshes and wet meadow-lands where it is often associated with cattle. It feeds on the insects disturbed by the grazing animals.

Pied wagtail (above)
and grey wagtail

Sedge Warbler *Acrocephalus schoenobaenus* Ceolaire
Cibe

A heavily streaked, brown warbler with a pronounced white streak over the eye. Its own song is harsh and unattractive, but it can mimic other birds. Feeds on insects, worms and spiders.
Where: Arrives in April or early May, having made a non-stop flight from the Sahara Desert. Common in wetlands throughout Ireland.

Grasshopper Warbler *Locustella naevia* Ceolaire
Casarnaí

A very shy bird, its presence is usually only indicated by its strange, penetrating reeling song (recalling the winding sound of an angler's reel), so high-pitched that older people may find it hard to hear.
Where: A common summer visitor, found in many different habitats.

Lesser Whitethroat *Sylvia curruca* Gilphib bheag
This bird rarely breeds in Ireland but is a common spring and autumn migrant as it passes from Europe to North Africa. Normally found in dense vegetation near coasts. Its diet is mostly insectivorous but it will eat berries in season.

Lesser whitethroat (above) and grasshopper warbler

Dartford Warbler *Sylvia undata* Ceolaire Fraoigh
An extremely rare autumn visitor, not often observed because of its skulking nature. You may observe one in areas of gorse, heather and brambles.

Whinchat *Saxicola rubetra* Caislín Aitinn
A small but brightly coloured bird. They can feed on spiders or worms but their main diet is insects.
Where: A summer migrant from Africa. They favour grassy tussocks for their nests, but can be found in many different locations, usually away from the coast.

Stonechat *Saxicola torquata* Caislín Cloch
This is the indigenous, resident cousin of the Whinchat. It derives its name from its song which recalls two small stones being knocked together.
Where: Found in most counties.

**Dartford warbler
(above) and whinchat**

Barn Owl *Tyto alba*   Scréachóg Reilige
Usually observed as a ghostly white outline in the
night, but can occasionally be seen at dusk. Its huge
eyes, penetrating the dark, silent wings and superb
hearing make it a deadly predator. Feeds on small
mammals and birds.
Where: Widespread farmland resident, but now scarce.

Snowy Owl *Nyctea scandiaca*
Sadly, a very rare visitor to this country. The male is
a huge, almost pure white owl which hunts by day.
The female has brown barring on its breast.

Long-eared Owl *Asio otus*   Ceann Cait
A secretive, nocturnal woodland owl. Usually the
best way to detect one is in the breeding season when
they emit their characteristic low, long hoot. Scarce,
but the commonest Irish owl.

Short-eared Owl *Asio flammeus*   Ulchabhán Réic
Can be observed hunting or roosting on the ground
during daylight hours. Typically, it flies only a few feet
in the air, gliding and hovering as it searches for its
prey.Normally a winter visitor but has bred in Ireland.

Barn owls

Pheasants

Pheasant *Phasianus colchicus*   Piasún
A large, impressive bird with a long barred tail. Very
noisy when disturbed, flying off with characteristic
whirring wing beats. Feeding normally on the
ground, its diet includes roots, seeds and berries.
Where: A common resident, breeding in all counties. To
be seen in farmland, woodland and upland scrub.

Red Grouse *Lagopus lagopus (hibernicus)*   Cearc
                                                  Fhraoigh
Red Grouse found in Ireland are generally paler than
the British variety and may well belong to a separate
species. Difficult to observe unless disturbed, when

they errupt noisily from the ground and fly off quickly. Feeds on heather shoots, flowers and seeds.
Where: Found all the year round on heather moorland.

Grey Partridge *Perdix perdix*   Patraisc
A shy, round game bird. Flies with quick, whirring wing beats, but more commonly runs for cover when startled. Often seen in small groups (coveys) feeding on seed, grain and insects.
Where: Once found in all counties, but now rare and only to be seen in farmland in the north and centre of Ireland.

Partridges

Jack snipe

Snipe *Gallinago gallinago*   Naoscach
A long-billed wader with creamy stripes on its head and back. During display flights in the spring, it spreads its outer tail feathers to create a strange 'drumming' sound which can be heard half a mile away. Its sensitive bill enables it to find worms in damp soil and mud.
Where: A common resident species, it nests on the ground in wetlands such as marshes, bogs and river shorelines.

Jack Snipe *Lymnocryptes minimus*   Naoscach
                                                    Bhídeach
A small wader. Distinguished from the Snipe by its shorter bill and more prominent back stripes. Excellent camouflage makes it hard to observe. It more often feeds off the surface of the water than the Snipe; its diet includes insects, worms, molluscs and seeds.
Where: A rare winter visitor found in wetlands.

Great Snipe *Gallinago media*   Naoscach
A rare visitor from northern Europe and Siberia. Slightly larger than the Snipe, it does not zigzag in flight.

Skylark *Alauda arvensis*   Fuiseog

Very rarely seen on the ground because of its excellent camouflage. It is easy to spot flying high in the sky and then hovering while it sings. It feeds on seeds, weeds, insects and worms.

Where: A year-round resident on farmland.

Shore Lark *Eremophila alpestris*
A large lark with a pale yellow face and dark eye-stripe. A gregarious bird which feeds on the ground, often keeping company with other larks.
Where: A very rare winter migrant from northern Europe. They can be found along the coast.

Peregrine falcons

Peregrine Falcon *Falco peregrinus*   Fabhcú gorm
A large impressive falcon with heavily barred wing feathers. During the last century the number of Peregrines declined appallingly; they have been persecuted by game keepers and many have been poisoned by pesticides especially DDT. Happily their population is, at last, beginning to increase. The falcon specialises in hunting birds, particularly those in flight. It circles at great heights and when it spots a victim folds back its wings and drops at great speed, striking the prey with its talons with such force that death is often instant.
Where: Residence widespread in coastal and mountainous areas.

Osprey *Pandion haliaetus*   Corineach
A large and beautiful raptor with a most striking appearance. Its white crown and underparts contrast spectacularly with its dark brown wings and back. At present, an uncommon passage migrant from Europe, but it is hoped that, as in Britain, it might soon begin to breed again in Ireland.
Where: Rare; mainly seen in coastal and lakeland areas.

Merlin *Falco columbarius*   Meirliún
A small, fast-flying falcon specialising in low-level
attacks on small birds. As with all hawks, the female
is larger than the male. It usually nests on the
ground.
Where: A scarce resident breeding species found throughout Ireland on heathland, moorland and hill farmland.

Kestrel *Falco tinnunculus*   Pocaire gaoithe
Often seen hovering in mid-air, it can be distinguished by its wedge-shaped tail. If you are lucky you
will see one suddenly swoop on its prey. Their diet is
mostly rodents and small birds but they will also feed
on worms and small insects.
Where: A common Irish bird found in a wide range of
habitats; can often be seen hovering near road verges.

Sparrowhawk *Accipiter nisus*   Spioróg
Probably the commonest Irish bird of prey. Using
the cover of bushes or hedges, it flies low over the
ground until it sees its prey, which it will then seize
with its large foot and carry off to tear and eat.
Where: Found throughout Ireland especially in woodland
and farmland with hedges and trees.

Kestrel

Buzzard *Buteo buteo*   Clamhán
A large and impressive predator. It is to be seen, wide
wings outstretched, gliding or hovering in search of its
prey. It enjoys a varied diet including rabbits, voles and
small birds. It may also feed on carrion.
Where: Can be found on farmland, mountains and
moorland in northern Ireland, but is not common
elsewhere.

Golden Eagle *Aquila chrysaetos*   Iolar mara
Sadly, it ceased to breed in Ireland at the beginning of
the century and now is only a rare visitor. It feeds on
small animals and birds, but, like the Buzzard, it can
also take carrion which makes it a prey to poison.

Hen Harrier *Circus cyaneus*   Cromán na gcearc
It has an elegant streamlined body and powerful,
narrow wings. Its underparts are white/light brown
and contrast vividly with the dark above. When
hunting, harriers cruise slowly a few feet above the
ground using their ears as much as their eyes to find
small birds or mammals concealed in the dense
vegetation below.
Where: Not common, but breeds in Ireland. Found on
mountains and heather moorlands.

Buzzard

Moorhen *Gallinula chloropus*   Cearc uisce
A very smart bird with bright red face and yellow
beak. It rarely dives for its food, preferring to feed
from the water surface. It can also be seen in
hedgerows and on fields, searching for snails and
insects.
Where: A widespread resident species living near
fresh water.

Coot *Accipiter nisus*   Spioróg
Easily recognised by its white forehead and bill. Often
found in groups, they are very territorial and aggres-
sive and spend much of their time squabbling.
Although they sometimes feed on land, Coots spend
most of their time on water where they dive for
aquatic plants and larvae.
Where: Common throughout Ireland in areas with lakes.

Water Rail *Rallus aquaticus*   Rálóg uisce
Very difficult to spot; the first indication of its
presence often being its distinctive repeated, loud,
squealing call. Its diet is mostly insects and small fish.
Where: A widespread resident species, found in
reedbeds, marshes and on river banks with dense
vegetation.

Moorhen

Ruff

Ruff *Philomachus pugnax*   Rufachán

Sadly a species much in decline now. Two hundred years ago they were much less scarce and a common table delicacy. The males would gather in their display areas puffing up their neck feathers in an attempt to intimidate their rivals: the darker the feathers, the more the females found them attractive. Its diet consists of worms, insects, crustaceons and molluscs.

Where: An uncommon migrant from Europe; found in wet, marshy places and low-lying pasture land.

Avocet *Recurvirostra avosetta*   Abhóiséad

A very striking black and white bird with a distinctive, turned-up black bill. They do not fidget in the mud with their beaks as do most other waders, but sweep their bills from side to side in the water, filtering out small insect larvae.

Where: Very scarce in Ireland nowadays, but can be found in estuaries and on mud flats during the winter.

Sanderling *Calidris alba*   Luathrán

A pretty little white bird with black legs and black flashes on the wings. Found round the coast where they can be seen at the water's edge chasing the waves up and down the beach.

Sandpiper

Curlew *Numenius arquata*   Crotach
A very large wader with brown specked covering and
a distinctive, long, down-turned bill with which it
probes for worms, insects, molluscs and crustacae.
Its long, mournful, rolling cry is often thought to
typify the bleak landscapes in which it lives.
Where: An increasingly common bird which nests on
moorland, farmland and damp meadows, but in
winter it moves to coastal grassland and estuaries.

Common Sandpiper *Actitis hypoleucos*   Gobadán
A small, neat wader, always on the move with its long
tail constantly bobbing up and down. It feeds on
insects, larvae, molluscs and tadpoles.
Where: A common species found on the edges of rocky
streams and rivers and on pebble and shingle beaches.

Black-tailed Godwit *Limosa limosa*   Guilbneach
                                              earrdhubh
Like its cousin the Bar-tailed Godwit, it is a common
winter visitor found in coastal areas and on mudflats
and estuaries. Godwits wade in deep water to feed
for shellfish and molluscs or take worms from soft
mud. Although similar in appearance, the two
species rarely mix.

Tufted Duck *Aythya fuligula*   Lacha bhadánach
The male is easily recognised by the tuft on the back of his black head, but the females are more drab with brown upper parts and paler belly. They are the deepest diving Irish ducks and can go down to twenty feet in their search for food.
Where: Found throughout Ireland on lakes and ponds, even those in city parks.

Eider *Somateria mollissima*
The male is a very beautiful black and white duck with black head, tail and wing tips and white face. They are 'sea ducks', as they spend most of their lives on the sea.
Where: Common on the northern coastline but rare elsewhere.

Mallard *Anas platyrhynchos*   Mallard

By far the most widespread duck in the world, the male has a beautiful glossy green head and a white collar. The female is a mottled brown. The chicks are particularly attractive, like little soft toys with yellow faces and fluffy brown backs. They like to feed while on water and can often be seen upended.

Where: Found throughout Ireland on lakes, ponds and estuaries.

Wigeon (left) and pochard

Wigeon *Anas penelope*   Lacha rua
A very gregarious bird; the male has a particularly striking orange/chestnut head and a high whistling call. *Where:* Few breed in Ireland, but they are a common winter visitor. Previously they lived almost entirely on eel-grass and were only seen on marshes and estuaries, but their diet has now widened and they can be found on inland lakes, gravel pits and grassland near to water.

Red-breasted Merganser *Mergus serrator* Siolta rua
A tufted duck with red bill, black head and white collar. It is a member of the sawbill family; so called because their bills have serrated edges to help them

catch and hold fish which they pursue under water.
Where: A common summer visitor which breeds on lakes and the larger rivers in the north and west of Ireland; winters by the coast.

Goosander *Mergus merganser*   Síolta mhór
The largest British sawbill. It has a blackish green head, red bill and white breast and flanks. Will sometimes nest in holes in trees; on water, the mother will carry her ducklings when she senses danger.
Where: A very rare summer visitor, found mostly in the north west on lakes and reservoirs.

Pochard *Aythya ferina*   Póiseard
A diving duck that can descend ten feet below the surface in search of aquatic vegetation. Outside the breeding season they usually flock together.
Where: A few pochard stay and breed in the summer but most are winter visitors from Europe. Found on ponds, lakes and in gravel pits.

Raven *Corvus corax*   Fiach dubh

It is the largest member of the crow family and is a glossy black from head to foot. In legend it is often associated with death, which is not surprising as it is a carrion eater and must have gathered at battle fields in the past. It will also kill and eat small mammals and birds and is an egg stealer.

Where: A common resident to be found in mountain valleys and on coastal cliffs.

Hooded Crow *Corvus coroni*   Feannóg

A large grey and black crow, which eats a wide range of food. It will feed on carrion, and will catch and kill small mammals and birds.

Where: A common resident bird which can be found in woodland, farmland, towns and coastal areas. You will sometimes see its cousin, the all-black Carrion Crow on a visit from Britain or Europe.

Jackdaw *Corvus monedula*   Cág

Glossy black with a grey nape. It has a penchant for shiny objects and this has given it its Latin name, *monedula* – 'little money bird'. An inquisitive and intelligent bird, it used to be popular as a pet because it could be taught a variety of tricks. It is fairly

Raven

Jay

omniverous, and has an unpleasant tendency to take eggs and infants from nests.

Where: Resident throughout Ireland and found in towns, woodland and on farmland. It can nest in chimneys and cause many problems for householders.

Magpie *Pica pica*   Snag breac

An easily recognised bird with its bright black and white plumage and long black tail. Its diet is wide and varied, but its habit of taking eggs and fledgelings has made it unpopular with many and perhaps given rise to the superstitions with which it is associated.

Where: It is thought to have arrived in Ireland in the mid-seventeenth century; the early colonists were very successful and quickly spread throughout the whole island. Found in towns and farmland.

Irish Jay *Garrulus glandarius*   Scréachóg

This is a different race from the British Jay, which is paler and has a whiter throat. Its habit of storing acorns, some of which it then forgets to reclaim, has helped to regenerate oaklands.

Bittern *Botaurus stellaris* Bonnán

A most impressive bird but now very rare and elusive. Even if you are lucky enough to hear its ominous boom you will be unlikely to find the bird. It is almost the size of a heron; well-built, speckled brown with a blackish crown.

Where: It overwinters in Ireland and can sometimes be observed in spring and early summer. Favours reedbeds.

Cormorant *Phalacrocorax carbo* Broigheal

A very tall bird; almost entirely black with just an occasional flash of white about the head and thigh. They are fish eaters and can dive for up to a minute while they search the bottom of shallow water for flat fish. Often seen standing still, with their wings outstretched; this may be to dry them, but no one is really sure why.

Where: Common all the year round. Once they stayed mainly in coastal districts but have now spread inland where they cause alarm among anglers who fear their effects on fish stocks.

Shag *Phalacrocorax aristotelis* Seaga

Like the Cormorant, but slightly smaller and crested. It fishes further out to sea and dives less deeply.

Bittern

Common Gull *Larus canus* Faoulieán bán

A medium-sized, resident gull; mostly white with
grey, black-tipped wings and black barred tail. It is not
right to think of it as a 'sea' gull; you are just as likely
to see it following a plough or searching a games field
as standing on a beach. Its diet is omniverous; you may
even spot it going through a rubbish tip for scraps.

Black-headed Gull *Larus ridibundus*   Sléibhín
A small gull with a white body, grey upperparts, and,
despite its name, a brown head. Like the common gull
it spends as much time inland as by the sea. It is also
omniverous and because it can adapt its diet to what is
available it is a very successful species. Breeds in large
colonies both on dunes and by freshwater pools.

Lapwing *Vanellus vanellus*   Pilbin

A large and very pretty plover often to be seen in flocks on meadowland throughout Ireland. It has a pronounced crest and white underparts; from a distance its wings appear black, but viewed more closely you will see they are a deep and subtle green. It is also called the Peewit from its distinctive cry, 'pee—wit'. The display flight of the male in early spring is most exciting: they fly high above their territory then tumble with humming wings until only a few feet above ground when they suddenly regain control of their flight. Feeds mostly on insects, snails and worms.

Woodcock *Scolopax rusticola*   Creabhar

Easily identified by its long, heavy bill, but well camouflaged and hard to spot in its native habitat. In the early breeding season the males can be seen 'roding', that is flying low over woodland while emitting their low call to attract a mate. It feeds on worms and insects which it finds in small pools or on damp ground.

Where: A resident breeding bird but joined by winter migrants from Europe. It is dispersed thinly through-out most of the country and is to be found in damp woodland.

Lapwings

Woodpigeon

Woodpigeon *Columba palumbus*   Colm coille
This is possibly the least popular bird in the whole of Ireland. Until recently it was only numerous in deciduous woodlands, but now it is common on farmland, where it is resented for its crop destruction, and in towns, where it is disliked for its shabby appearance and ubiquitous droppings. Its wide range of diet and readiness to adapt to new circumstances probably account for its success.
Where: A resident species widely scattered throughout the country.

Corncrake *Crex crex*   Traonach
In the last century the Corncrake was common throughout Ireland, but now it is an endangered species found only in a very few sites. A combination of factors account for its decline: climatic change in Africa where it winters; the fact that it flies at low altitude when migrating and often collides with power lines; and farmers cutting grass early in the year for silage destroy its nests. It is a very shy bird and its loud call ('crex, crex', from which it derives its Latin name) is often the only clue to its presence.
Where: Found in meadowlands and areas of tall vegetation.

Dipper *Cinclus cinclus hibernicus*   Gabha dubh
Peculiar to Ireland this race of dipper has a dark back
and wide chestnut band on its breast. Found on the
banks of fast-flowing streams it will often dive for fish.